INTRODUCTION

Dinosaurs dominated the Earth for more than 150 million years, and they've been an endless source of fascination since they were first discovered. Traces of their existence have been preserved in stone, and new ones are being dug up every day.

The constant discoveries about dinosaurs are revolutionizing what we know about animal life. In this book, we'll follow in the footsteps of paleontologists on an adventure through this fascinating world!

First, we'll learn what a fossil is, and where the main fossil sites are found on our planet. Then, we'll take a look at the timeline and find out how the continents were formed. This will give us a better idea about the world the dinosaurs lived in.

Finally, we'll find out how the first dinosaurs appeared and follow these terrible lizards on their journey, from their peak to their slow decline and their ultimate disappearance.

TABLE OF CONTENTS

FOSSILS

What is a fossil?

A fossil is the remains of a plant or an animal preserved naturally in the ground. When plants and animals die, they usually decompose and disappear into the soil. But under precise conditions and over time, the remains form fossils, which can be quite difficult to find.

The Bone Wars

In the late 1800s, Edward Cope and Charles Marsh, two well-known American paleontologists, competed to find fossils in a race known as the Bone Wars, or the Great Dinosaur Rush. Together, they discovered more than 120 new dinosaur species!

How fossils are formed

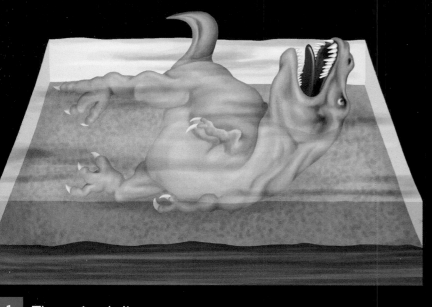

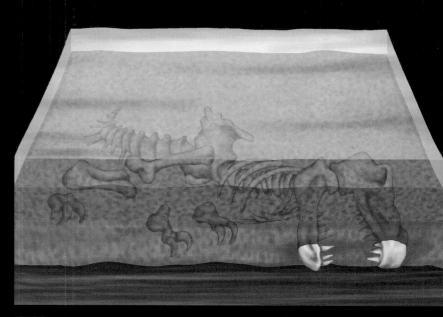

1 The animal dies.

2 Its body is covered with sediment and decomposes.

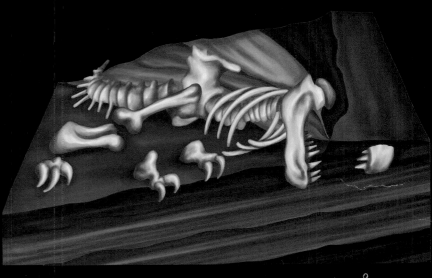

3 The sediment is transformed into solid sedimentary rock, which contains traces of the animal.

4 The movements of the Earth's crust bring the fossils to the surface.

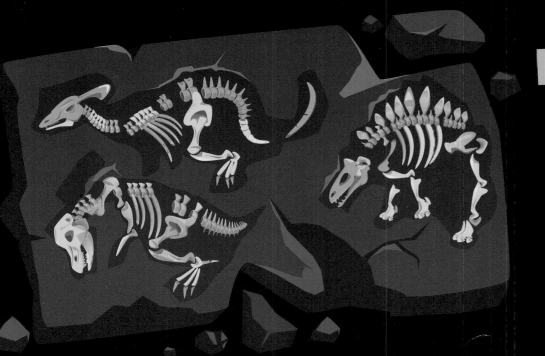

Geology 101

Depending on how they are formed, rocks are divided into three families: igneous, sedimentary and metamorphic.

Fossils are usually found in sedimentary rocks, which are made up of layers of particles covering the remains of plants and animals.

A PALEONTOLOGIST'S WORK

Paleontologists hunt for remnants of the past buried under the ground. But how do they know where to look and what tools to use?

Where to look

When deciding where to dig, paleontologists first study the topography of the land.

They often work with a geologist, who knows all about rocks. For example, cliffs and deserts are good places to look for fossils.

Paleontologists also look for spots where the rock is already exposed.

DID YOU KNOW?

People have been finding gigantic bones in the ground for thousands of years. Before realizing they belonged to animals that had since gone extinct, they were believed to be the remains of giants or even mythical creatures like dragons! Some 2,500 years ago, people believed that stones resembling animal parts were pieces in a mysterious game.

Paleontology tools

Paleontologists use different tools to dig for fossils. A hammer and chisel are used to chip away at rocks located on the surface. Once the fossil is exposed, paleontologists prefer to use stiff brushes, scrapers, and needles. They also use special glue to preserve the fragile pieces.

PRESERVING FOSSILS

The study of fossils

Each piece that's unearthed is bagged and labeled. This is a very important step because thousands of fossils are sometimes found at the same site.

The labels contain vital information, such as where the fossil was found and at what depth, the soil composition, and the date.

Everything is then shipped to the lab, where the paleontologist finishes cleaning and cataloging the fossils. They use a magnifying glass, special lights, a scanner, and other instruments to identify the species.

Based on their findings, the paleontologist can match pieces of the same animal found several yards apart. Finally, they try to figure out what the animal might have looked like.

At the museum

The next time you visit a museum, you may see real prehistoric animal bones on display. But most of the big fossils in museums are casts—the bones are copies of the real ones made out of plaster, which is stronger, lighter, and easier to maintain.

DISCOVERIES AROUND THE WORLD

A fossil site is a place where many species have been preserved. There are many spots around the world brimming with the fossilized remains of prehistoric animals.

In the United States, some sites have yielded important information about several well-known dinosaurs, such as *Tyrannosaurus rex*, *Allosaurus*, and *Stegosaurus*.

Argentina is the uncontested champion in South America with 131 species found!

Four dinosaur species have been discovered in Antarctica.

DID YOU KNOW?

Argentina's Ischigualasto Provincial Park is a huge fossil site for all kinds of vertebrates, including dinosaurs! It's known as the Valley of the Moon, because its gray-and-white landscape looks a lot like Earth's satellite.

Germany and Belgium are the two European countries where the most fossils have been found.

In China's Yunnan province, many fossils have been discovered at the Chengjiang Fossil Site, which is made up of shale, a layered rock that flakes apart in thin sheets.

Many fossils can be found in Asia—more than 340 species of dinosaurs have been discovered there.

Africa's Sahara Desert contains extensive fossil sites, where no fewer than 73 species have been discovered.

EVOLUTION OF THE CONTINENTS

The shape of the continents has changed a lot over time. North and South America, Africa, Europe, and Asia as we know them today did not always exist. Despite their massive size, the continents have drifted over millions of years. However slow, they are always on the move.

Have you ever wondered why dinosaur fossils of the same species have been found in different parts of the world? The answer is simple: Back when the supercontinent Pangaea existed, the creatures could roam all over the planet. Then, Pangaea broke up into two main continents, Laurasia and Gondwana, which later drifted apart and eventually split up into the continents we know today.

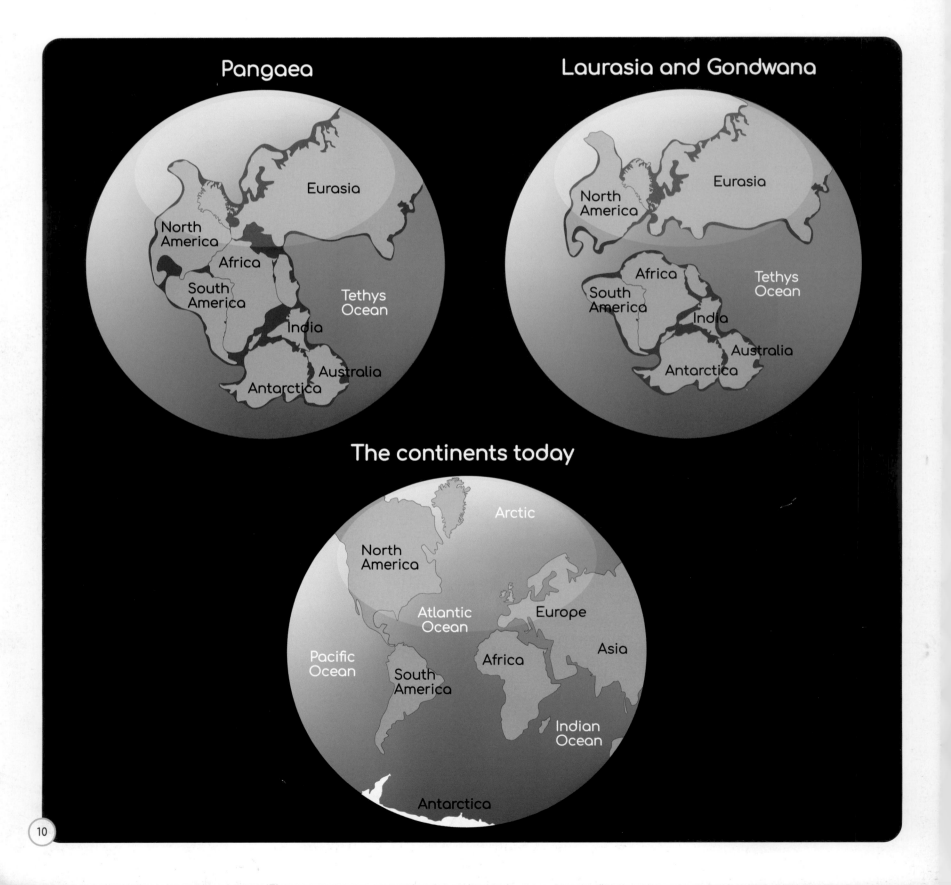

TIMELINE

Scientists are able to study the history of the Earth and its inhabitants, from the time our planet was first formed, using a timeline known as the geologic time scale. Since we know that dinosaurs no longer exist, this timeline helps us figure out when different plant and animal species lived.

The history of the Earth can be divided into four eras: the Precambrian, the Paleozoic, the Mesozoic, and the Cenozoic. These eras can be further subdivided into different periods. For example, the Mesozoic era is made up of the Triassic, Jurassic, and Cretaceous periods.

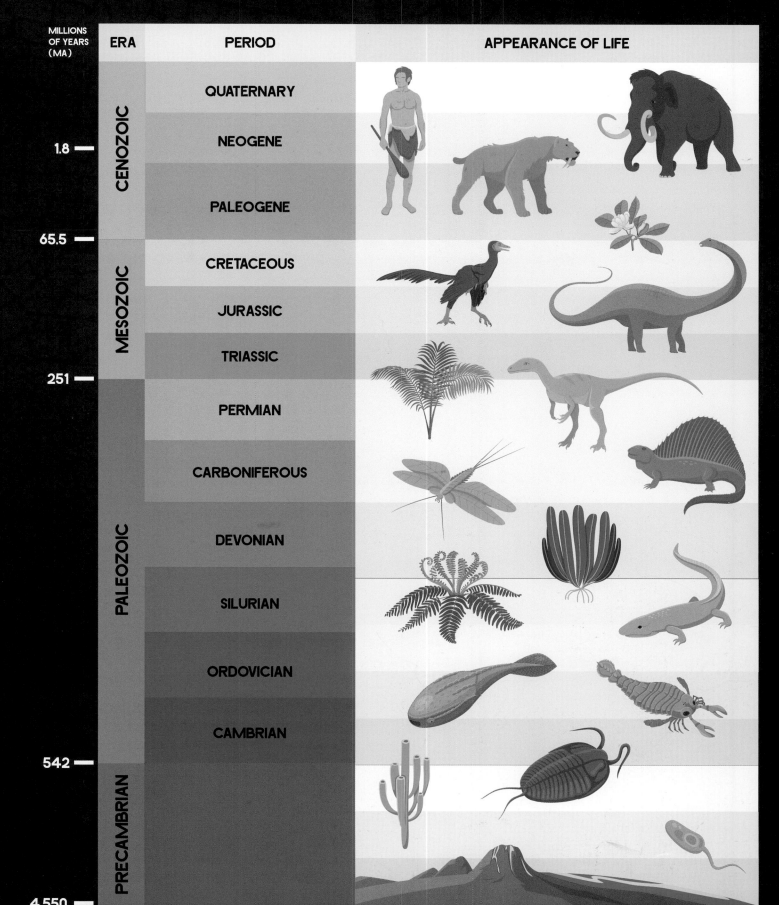

MILLIONS OF YEARS (MA)	ERA	PERIOD	APPEARANCE OF LIFE
	CENOZOIC	QUATERNARY	
1.8		NEOGENE	
		PALEOGENE	
65.5	MESOZOIC	CRETACEOUS	
		JURASSIC	
		TRIASSIC	
251	PALEOZOIC	PERMIAN	
		CARBONIFEROUS	
		DEVONIAN	
		SILURIAN	
		ORDOVICIAN	
		CAMBRIAN	
542	PRECAMBRIAN		
4,550			

THE GEOLOGIC ERAS

The Earth was formed about 4.6 billion years ago. The four known geologic eras each had different living conditions that led to the appearance of life. Here is an overview:

THE PRECAMBRIAN ERA

The earliest era of Earth's history.

TIMELINE

From 4.55 billion years ago
to 542 million years ago

PERIODS

None

EVENT MARKING THE BEGINNING OF THE ERA

Formation of the Earth and other planets in the solar system

LAYOUT OF THE CONTINENTS

Pangaea

PLANT AND ANIMAL SPECIES PRESENT

First life forms: bacteria + single-celled and multicelled organisms (cyanobacteria and stromatolites)

THE PALEOZOIC ERA

The second era of Earth's history.

TIMELINE

From 542 million years ago
to 251 million years ago

PERIODS

Cambrian, Ordovician, Silurian, Devonian, Carboniferous, and Permian

EVENT MARKING THE BEGINNING OF THE ERA

Appearance of invertebrates

LAYOUT OF THE CONTINENTS

Pangaea

PLANT AND ANIMAL SPECIES PRESENT

- First invertebrates with a shell: bivalves and trilobites
- First vertebrates: *Pikaia* (ancestor of reptiles, dinosaurs, birds, and mammals)
- First land-dwelling organisms: amphibians and reptiles that later evolved into dinosaurs (*Dimetrodon* and *Eryops*)

THE MESOZOIC ERA

The third era of Earth's history.

TIMELINE

From 251 million years ago
to 65.5 million years ago

PERIODS

Triassic, Jurassic, and Cretaceous

EVENT MARKING
THE BEGINNING OF THE ERA

Appearance of the first dinosaurs

LAYOUT OF THE CONTINENTS

Laurasia and Gondwana (end of the Jurassic period)

PLANT AND ANIMAL
SPECIES PRESENT

- Dinosaurs
- First mammals
- Diversification of plants to flowers

THE CENOZOIC ERA

The fourth era of Earth's history,
and the one we are currently in today.

TIMELINE

From 65.5 million years ago
to today

PERIODS

Paleogene, Neogene, and Quaternary

EVENT MARKING
THE BEGINNING OF THE ERA

Extinction of the dinosaurs
and several other species

LAYOUT OF THE CONTINENTS

As we know them today

PLANT AND ANIMAL
SPECIES PRESENT

Appearance of most known species of birds,
insects, mammals, fish, and plants

THE TRANSITION TO THE DINOSAUR ERA

Dinosaurs no longer exist. Fossils are all that is left of their time on Earth.

How did the first dinosaurs appear?

Paleontologists have found fossils dating back as far as 252 million years, from the Permian period, in the late Paleozoic era. The oldest dinosaur fossils ever found are those of *Euparkeria* and *Herrerasaurus*, fearsome reptiles thought to have evolved from archosaurs, or "giant lizards."

Archosaur

Herrerasaurus

The start of the dinosaur era

At the end of the Paleozoic era, more than 95% of marine species and 70% of land-dwelling species were wiped out in a mass extinction. This event marked the beginning of the Mesozoic era, paving the way for the appearance and diversification of dinosaurs.

DID YOU KNOW?

In 2003, geologist Jean Boissonnas discovered a site in Switzerland chock full of fossilized footprints. These footprints are believed to belong to archosaurs, a family of creatures older than the dinosaurs.

CATEGORIES OF DINOSAURS

To date, roughly 900 species of dinosaurs have been identified.

Mapping the dinosaurs' family tree can be a challenge since not all paleontologists agree on the best way to classify the ancient animals. What they do agree on is that all dinosaurs that ever existed fall into two main categories: **saurischians** and **ornithischians**. The main difference between the two was the structure of their pelvic bones.

Saurischians

The pelvic bones of saurischians looked a lot like those of reptiles, such as lizards and crocodiles. There were two main types of saurischians: **theropods** and **sauropodomorphs**.

TYPE	MAIN CHARACTERISTICS	EXAMPLES	PRESENCE DURING THE MESOZOIC ERA
Theropods	Bipedal carnivores	*Archaeopteryx* and *Tyrannosaurus rex*	Triassic ✓ Jurassic ✓ Cretaceous ✓
Sauropodomorphs	Long-necked, quadruped herbivores	Sauropods (*Brachiosaurus* and *Titanosaurus*)	Triassic ✓ Jurassic ✓ Cretaceous ✓

Ornithischians

The pelvic bones of ornithischians were very similar to those of birds. There were three main types of ornithischians: **ornithopods**, **thyreophorans**, and **marginocephalians**.

TYPE	MAIN CHARACTERISTICS	EXAMPLES	PRESENCE DURING THE MESOZOIC ERA
Ornithopods	Bipedal herbivores with many teeth and a duckbill-shaped beak	*Heterodontosaurus* and *Parasaurolophus*	Triassic ✗ Jurassic ✓ Cretaceous ✓
Thyreophorans	Quadruped herbivores with bony plates or spikes on their backs	*Stegosaurus* and *Ankylosaurus*	Triassic ✗ Jurassic ✓ Cretaceous ✓
Marginocephalians	Quadruped herbivores with one or more horns	*Triceratops*	Triassic ✗ Jurassic ✓ Cretaceous ✓

THE MESOZOIC ERA: THE AGE OF DINOSAURS

The Mesozoic era was truly the age of dinosaurs. During this time, a large number of species appeared and quickly diversified to inhabit the land, seas, and skies all over the planet.

There's no question about it: During this time, dinosaurs ruled the Earth! As you know, the Mesozoic era is divided into three periods: the Triassic, Jurassic, and Cretaceous.

TRIASSIC PERIOD

The Triassic is the earliest period of the Mesozoic era. At the time, Earth was made up of a single, gigantic supercontinent called Pangaea, which literally means "the entire Earth." The Triassic period spanned more than 51 million years. During this period, Pangaea started to break up, giving rise to two enormous continents: Gondwana and Laurasia.

Eurasia

North America

Africa

South America

Tethys Ocean

India

Australia

Antarctica

JURASSIC PERIOD

During the Jurassic period, the continents broke apart for good. The transition from the Triassic period to the Jurassic period saw the disappearance of approximately 50% of life on Earth. This is when the dinosaurs were at their peak.

CRETACEOUS PERIOD

During the Cretaceous period, the continents drifted farther apart. The period began with a significant decline in marine life and a huge diversification of terrestrial life forms. It ended with the mass extinction of the dinosaurs.

THE TRIASSIC PERIOD: APPEARANCE OF THE DINOSAURS

The Triassic was a period of profound change and huge diversification of life on Earth. The first dinosaurs appeared during this period. But they weren't the giants you imagine: The first dinosaurs were actually small.

The climate

The climate was very different from today's. The lands in the middle of Pangaea were so far away from the oceans that rain was very rare. The center of the supercontinent was made up of vast deserts. For that reason, life was mainly concentrated on the coasts, where the temperature was milder and the air more humid. Most plant life also grew in these coastal areas.

The vegetation

The vegetation already looked a lot like it does today. Many types of ferns were very common, especially in swampy areas, but flowers didn't yet exist.

Insects and arthropods

The high amount of oxygen in the air allowed insects to grow to enormous sizes.

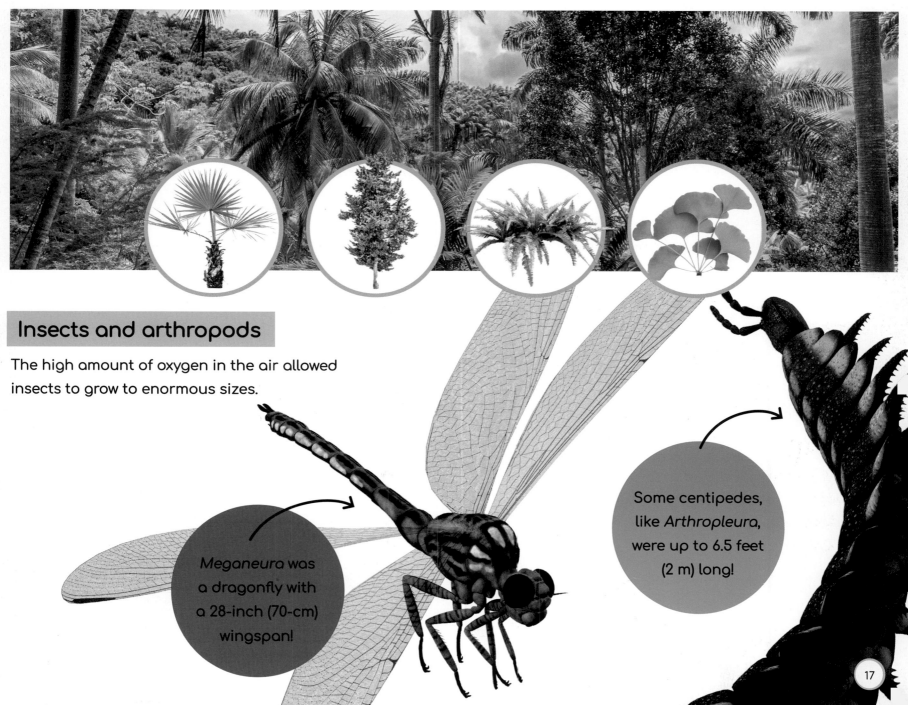

Meganeura was a dragonfly with a 28-inch (70-cm) wingspan!

Some centipedes, like *Arthropleura*, were up to 6.5 feet (2 m) long!

THE FIRST DINOSAURS

Coelophysis

This dinosaur lived mainly in the desert plains.

It was an ancestor of the great prehistoric predators, the theropods.
It was a carnivore and an excellent hunter.

Its powerful legs ended in three toes tipped with long claws.
It also had a fourth, tiny toe that never touched the ground.

Its hands had three long fingers and one very short one.
These helped it to capture and hold onto its prey.

Its thin snout was characteristic of predators that fed mainly on small animals.

Interestingly, its curved front teeth pointed backward. This helped it capture
small animals. Its other teeth were serrated like steak knives.

Eoraptor lunensis

Eoraptor is one of the dinosaurs whose fossilized remains were found in Ischigualasto, an archaeological site in northwestern Argentina.

Its name means "dawn thief."

Discovered in 1991, it is one of the oldest known dinosaurs.

Eoraptor is a saurischian, like the theropods and sauropods.
But its overall shape is closer to that of the theropods.

The *Eoraptor* teeth that have been found suggest that it was an omnivore.
It may have eaten plants, like the sauropods, and meat, like the theropods.

Its front teeth, which it used to grind up leaves, were wide and flat.
The back ones were pointed and curved to tear apart meat.

This small dinosaur measured about 5 feet (1.5 m).
It's thought to have been a very fast hunter of small lizards or even small mammals.

Plateosaurus

Plateosaurus lived in the forests and swamps of the Triassic period. It is the ancestor of the sauropodomorphs, long-necked dinosaurs. It walked on two legs, and its five-toed feet probably helped it to run really fast.

It had four fingers and a thumb on each hand, which it used to hold onto its food.

Its eyes were located on the sides of its head, giving it a wide field of vision. It could see its enemies long before they got too close!

Plateosaurus preferred to live in groups.

Cynodontia

Cynodontia was a furry reptile with its legs positioned under its body, like modern mammals. At the time, the distinction between reptiles and mammals wasn't as clear as it is today.

Paleontologists have discovered many small pits in *Cynodontia*'s skull, which are thought to have contained nerves connected to whiskers. *Cynodontia* may have been warm-blooded, meaning it produced heat to keep its body at a constant temperature.

Cynodontia also had a hard palate, which allowed it to breathe and eat at the same time!

Rhynchosaur

Rhynchosaur was a strange reptile with a parrot-like beak that lived during the late Triassic period. Many fossils of this herbivore have been found.

Rhynchosaur's teeth were very unique. It had several rows of teeth, which didn't grow back after falling out. This reptile eventually gave rise to mammals.

IN THE TRIASSIC SKY

All prehistoric flying reptiles were pterosaurs belonging to the category of ornithischians. They first appeared during the Triassic period, when they ruled the skies. Unlike reptiles, which are normally cold-blooded, meaning they use the heat from their environment to control their body temperature, pterosaurs were warm-blooded. That's why they had enough energy left over to fly!

Another thing that made pterosaurs unique was their hollow bones. This made them much lighter, giving them a huge advantage when it came to flying!

Eudimorphodon

One of the oldest pterosaurs, *Eudimorphodon* was about the size of a crow. And it didn't just glide: It actually flew by flapping its wings!

Eudimorphodon's wings were made up of a membrane supported by the arm bone and a very long finger. A small fin at the end of its tail probably helped it steer.

IN THE TRIASSIC SEAS

The marine reptiles of the Triassic period were the descendants of land-dwelling reptiles that returned to the water. As they evolved, they kept certain features from their time on dry land. They appeared in the seas at the same time as dinosaurs appeared on land.

Nothosaur

Nothosaur was a prehistoric marine reptile with legs that it used to swim.

Its long, flexible neck allowed it to move quickly, and its jaw was lined with many short, pointy teeth. These features were ideal for catching small fish.

It is believed that *Nothosaur* stayed close to the shore, resting there when it wasn't hunting. Its webbed feet allowed it to walk on the beaches.

Its short legs prevented
it from hunting on the ground.
But its muscles allowed it to change
the shape of its wings during flight.
This characteristic meant that
Eudimorphodon could catch
its prey by skimming along
the surface of the water.

Ichthyosaur

Ichthyosaur was also a prehistoric marine reptile, but it didn't have feet—only fins.
This meant it was unable to walk on land. The female gave birth
underwater once her babies were fully developed inside her.
The babies knew how to swim from the minute
they were born.

Ichthyosaur's body
was very aerodynamic,
like a dolphin. It used
the same left-to-right
wiggling motion
to swim.

THE JURASSIC PERIOD: THE PEAK OF THE DINOSAUR ERA

A diverse range of life-forms appeared early on during the Jurassic period, including several of the biggest, most massive dinosaur species. The dinosaurs reached their peak during this period, with large numbers of species roaming the planet side by side.

The climate

When Pangaea broke up, forming the two continents of Laurasia and Gondwana, any land masses ended up next to water. Many places that were previously dry were suddenly humid. But the temperature was still warm. This led to an abundance of plant life in the tropical Tethys Ocean—an ideal food source for many animals.

The vegetation

The plants of the Jurassic period were a lot like those of the Triassic period. There were still no flowers, but the warm, damp forests were the perfect breeding grounds for ferns. Conifers, or evergreens, also made their appearance alongside plants that looked like palm trees.

Other animals

During the Jurassic period, mammals started to look more and more different from reptiles, but were still small. Insects, on the other hand, grew to impressive sizes compared to their modern descendants. There was also an explosion in the numbers and types of other invertebrates, in the water, on land, and in the air.

Megazostrodon

DID YOU KNOW?

Jurassic National Monument, in Utah, contains the densest concentration of Jurassic dinosaur fossils ever found—more than 12,000 bones. This represents roughly 74 different dinosaurs! Several *Allosaurus* fossils have been found at different stages of life, giving paleontologists a snapshot of how this big carnivore might have lived.

ARRIVAL OF THE GIANTS: THE SAUROPODOMORPHS

The sauropodomorphs were saurischian herbivores.
They were quadrupeds that all had a long neck and an even longer tail!

Anatomy of a sauropodomorph

A sauropodomorph's long neck allowed it to eat leaves straight from the treetops. Some species were so tall that the blood didn't make it to their head if they raised it too high!

Their long tail did not drag on the ground.

Their front legs had short toes with only one bone each.

Their hind legs were very strong because they had to support the full weight of the animal.

Sauropodomorph fossils

The long, fragile skeletons of sauropodomorphs are very hard to unearth without breaking them. And their skulls are rarely found with the rest of the bones.

The oldest specimen found is *Isanosaurus*, from Thailand. It lived at the end of the Triassic period.

Sauropods

One of the biggest groups of sauropodomorphs, sauropods are classified into two groups according to the shape of their teeth: **brachiosaurs** and **diplodocids**.

- **Brachiosaurs** are sauropods with spoon-shaped teeth.

Brachiosaurus

Brachiosaurus had longer front legs than back legs. Located at the end of its very long neck, its head was more than 43 feet (13 m) off the ground!

Brachiosaurus ate leaves, which it picked off the trees with its teeth. Oddly enough, its nostrils were bigger than its eye sockets!

Giraffatitan

This African dinosaur used to be known as *Brachiosaurus*, like its American cousin—until paleontologists realized they were too different to be the same species. It's estimated to have weighed between 50 and 85 tons!

Sauroposeidon

Sauroposeidon was the biggest of the brachiosaurs, at nearly 100 feet (30 m) long.

Diplodocus

At 80 feet (25 m) long, *Diplodocus* was one of the biggest dinosaurs that ever lived! What made *Diplodocus* so unique was its extremely long tail made up of 73 vertebrae and ending in a whip. As there were no muscles in its tail, it wasn't strong enough to hit other dinosaurs with. But the sharp sound it made would have definitely scared them off!

Well-preserved fossils tell us that *Diplodocus* had spines from head to tail.

DID YOU KNOW
that the sauropods in the movie *The Good Dinosaur* are Apatosauruses?

Apatosaurus

Apatosaurus is also known as *Brontosaurus*. Despite being shorter than the other diplodocids, it became famous for the controversy it caused when paleontologists discovered that the fossilized bones of *Apatosaurus* and *Brontosaurus*, which they thought were two different species, were actually identical.

29

RULE OF THE SAURISCHIANS: THE BIG THEROPODS

The saurischians were one of the two main categories of dinosaurs. Theropods were two-legged saurischian dinosaurs that were almost all carnivores.

History of the theropods

The oldest theropod is *Eoraptor*, which lived during the Triassic period. The most famous is *Tyrannosaurus rex*, which lived during the Cretaceous period.

Physiology of theropods

Armed with powerful jaws and sharp teeth, theropods tore the flesh off their prey. Some theropods had cone-shaped teeth that looked more like a crocodile's teeth; paleontologists have decided that these species ate fish. Theropods had small front legs tipped with long, sharp claws, which they used like knives to shred their prey.

Its extendable jaw could stretch to fit bigger pieces of meat. Paleontologists know that *Allosaurus* hunted *Stegosaurus* because holes were found in a fossilized *Stegosaurus* plate that were an exact match to the big carnivore's teeth.

Types of theropods

Many theropods were gigantic and couldn't chase their victims because they were too heavy. For that reason, they staked out their prey, waiting for an unsuspecting herbivore to happen by.

Other theropods were small and fast. Based on fossilized footprints, paleontologists have calculated that some could run as fast as 30 miles (50 km) per hour—the average running speed of a tiger! Because they were small, their bones were more fragile, so fossils are less common.

Allosaurus

During the Jurassic period, the most fearsome dinosaur in North America was definitely *Allosaurus*. Unlike other theropods, it had strong arms capable of holding onto its prey. *Allosaurus* was slender, which allowed it to run. Its eyes, located under small horns, looked out to the side instead of forward, like most predators.

Compsognathus

Compsognathus was the smallest theropod of the Jurassic period, at just 3 feet (1 m)—the size of a big turkey!

A fast hunter with excellent eyesight, it ate lizards, insects, and even small mammals. One fossil even contained the full skeleton of a lizard that *Compsognathus* swallowed whole!

But not a lot is known about these small theropods because their hollow bones often disappeared before they could be turned into fossils.

Cryolophosaurus

Cryolophosaurus is famous for having been discovered on the continent of Antarctica, where the climate was mild during the Jurassic period. This lightweight theropod had a crest that ran across the top of its head from side to side, above its eyes. This was probably a feature used to attract potential partners during the mating ritual.

Megalosaurus

Megalosaurus was king of the dinosaurs in Europe. At 10 feet (3 m) tall, it had short, but strong arms, and powerful jaws that its prey had no chance of escaping from. *Megalosaurus* was the first dinosaur to be given a scientific name, in 1824.

ORNITHISCHIANS EVERYWHERE: UNOBTRUSIVE HERBIVORES

Ornithischians were the second main category of dinosaurs. Many quadruped herbivores with beak-shaped mouths roamed the Earth during the Jurassic period.

Heterodontosaurus

This small herbivore, an ornithopod, had three types of teeth, which was quite rare for that time. Mammals typically have incisors, canines, and molars, which is why paleontologists think that *Heterodontosaurus* might have been an omnivore rather than just an herbivore.
Its large eyes suggest that it was a nocturnal animal. Its body was probably covered with down similar to primitive feathers.

Kentrosaurus

This African thyreophoran measured only 16 feet (5 m).
Like its cousin *Stegosaurus*, *Kentrosaurus* had bony plates.
But halfway down its back, these were replaced with long backward-pointing spikes. Its tail was very flexible, which allowed *Kentrosaurus* to swing it quickly at enemies.

Scelidosaurus

This 13-foot-long (4-m) armored thyreophoran also had protective plates. It was a quadruped that could run on two legs when needed. Its teeth were used to crush its food, but not to chew.

Stegosaurus

This 30-foot-long (9-m) thyreophoran had bony plates from its neck to its tail. These plates could grow up to 6.5 feet (2 m) tall! They may have been used to regulate the dinosaur's body temperature. One thing is certain: They made Stegosaurus appear bigger and scarier to its predators.

During combat, Stegosaurus did not use its plates, which were very fragile. Instead, it defended itself with the spikes at the end of its flexible tail. Despite being massive, Stegosaurus had a tiny brain.

IN THE JURASSIC SKY

The primitive pterosaurs that filled the Triassic sky evolved during the Jurassic period, but they stayed small. However, they were no longer alone in the sky: The first bird made its appearance, along with other flying dinosaurs!

Archaeopteryx

The earliest known bird, *Archaeopteryx* was an ornithischian that appeared during the Jurassic period. It was quickly followed by other bird species. But what made it different was that it was closely related to the dinosaurs. Its discovery changed our understanding of the link between reptiles and birds. And yet, only about a dozen *Archaeopteryx* fossils have ever been found!

It's believed that *Archaeopteryx*'s feathers evolved from the soft down that grew on theropods at that time. Unlike the feathered dinosaurs, the dromaeosaurs, the feathers on *Archaeopteryx*'s wings were made for flight. Its long legs would have allowed it to take off by leaping off the ground.

IN THE JURASSIC SEAS

Many different marine reptiles swam the Jurassic seas. They had lungs, which meant they had to rise to the surface regularly to breathe. They were not the only creatures in the Jurassic seas. A huge number of fossilized plants and animals have been found in layers of sedimentary rock from this period.

Ammonoids

Fossils reveal that ammonites had spiral shells. More than 5,000 different species of this mollusk have been identified. They varied in size from a few inches to several feet in diameter.

Ammonites had several long, powerful tentacles emerging from the opening at one end of their shell. They also had many eyes.

Archaeopteryx could not fly long distances because its bone structure was not made to support its weight.

Dimorphodon

This prehistoric flying reptile had a very peculiar feature: Its skull was enormous. It had a highly developed sense of vision and movement—as much as today's birds.

Plesiosaurs and Pliosaurs

Plesiosaurus and *Pliosaurus* were descendants of marine predators.

These fish lovers swam with the aid of wing-like paddles that were neither legs nor flippers.

Plesiosaurs had a long neck and a small head, whereas P*liosaurus* had a shorter neck but a massive head.

THE CRETACEOUS PERIOD: DIVERSIFICATION OF THE DINOSAURS

The Jurassic period ended with a mass extinction, an event that had a profound impact on marine life. The Cretaceous period followed, and because the planet was divided into two continents, Laurasia and Gondwana, life forms evolved differently in different parts of the world. More and more unusual dinosaurs began to appear.

The climate

During the Cretaceous period, the continents began to slowly drift apart, gradually taking shape as the ones we know today, in the Cenozoic era. Different parts of the planet developed their own particular climates. The amount of coastal areas increased, giving rise to more wetlands. The climate was mostly warm, but the movement of land masses toward the poles would slowly lead to a drop in temperature all over the planet.

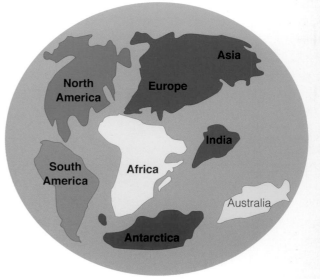

The vegetation

Increasingly diversified woodlands were beginning to spread across the continents. Flowering plants appeared alongside ferns, conifers, and ginkgo plants. Competition for space heated up between conifers and deciduous trees. Graminids, or grasses, also appeared on the ground. Herbivores during this period had a much wider selection of food than before.

Other animals

Invertebrates that fed on nectar finally appeared, since there were now flowers in need of pollinators. Mammals became much more diverse than reptiles, while in the water, sharks emerged to compete with the big marine reptiles.

DID YOU KNOW?
The Cretaceous period also ended with a huge mass extinction that led to the disappearance of almost all the dinosaurs as we know them.

BIRD FEET: THE ORNITHOPODS

The ornithopods, whose name means "bird feet," were dinosaurs with feet shaped very much like a bird's. They belong to the category of ornithischians and are also well-known for having a duckbill-shaped beak.

Iguanodon

About the size of an elephant, this dinosaur was nicknamed the "cow of the Cretaceous period," because traces of many herds have been found on the fertile plains of several different continents.

Iguanodon's skull looked like that of a horse. It had a beak perfect for grazing grass and teeth with sharp edges for chewing leaves. It stood on its back legs to eat the leaves straight off the trees.

Iguanodon's front legs were long enough to touch the ground. But they were shaped more like arms, with a thumb the dinosaur could use to defend itself.

Iguanodon was one of the first dinosaurs described in the 1800s. Since paleontology was a new science at the time, it was hard for scientists to determine what *Iguanodon* might have looked like. At first, the remains were thought to belong to a crawling lizard. Then paleontologists thought it might have used its tail for balance, like a kangaroo. Finally, they decided that *Iguanodon* was a quadruped that held its tail off the ground.

• **Hadrosaurs** are a family of duck-billed dinosaurs. Their ancestors were similar to *Iguanodon* and they had hundreds of tiny teeth. It's believed that they also lived in herds. Many of them also had strange crests on their heads.

Corythosaurus

Its plate-shaped crest looked like the helmets worn by ancient Roman soldiers.

Edmontosaurus

This quadruped's back legs were much bigger and stronger than its arms.

It had a bigger beak than the other species.

Maiasaura

Several fossilized Maiasaura nests have been found next to each other, leading paleontologists to believe that these dinosaurs laid their eggs in the same place. They probably fed their babies right in their nests—rare proof of dinosaur parents taking care of their young.

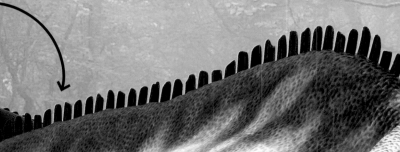

Parasaurolophus

Parasaurolophus had a long, backward-facing crest on top of its head. Paleontologists think the dinosaur used it to amplify its cries.

BONY TANKS: THE THYREOPHORANS

Some dinosaurs were stocky and had bodies covered with plates and spines. The thyreophorans were ornithischians that appeared during the Jurassic period, but they reached their peak during the Cretaceous period. They were divided into two large families: **nodosaurids** and **ankylosaurids**. The main difference between them was that ankylosaurids had a club at the end of their tail.

Euoplocephalus

The four bony plates on this ankylosaurid's tail fused together to form a huge, solid club, which it used to defend itself against predators that dared to attack.

Its skull was covered with thick bones to protect its brain. It even had bony eyelids to keep its eyes safe. With all that armor, it moved along slowly, without much of a thought to the giant carnivores.

Gastonia

This dinosaur was covered in so many spines that it looked like a thorny bush. It had sideways spikes on its tail, two rows of spikes on its back, and spines all over the rest of its body. *Gastonia*'s tail didn't end in a club, but it was still dangerous, because the dinosaur used it like a whip.

Sauropelta

This nodosaurid was covered in huge pieces of bone attached with very small plates. Because its belly was not protected and it had short legs, it often dropped to the ground to protect itself.

LITTLE RUNNERS: THE QUICK THEROPODS

During the Cretaceous period, the big carnivores were not the only creatures to be feared. The jungles, forests and savannas were populated by smaller—but faster and more agile—predators.

Oviraptor

Oviraptor was probably the closest theropod to a bird. It measured 5 feet (1.5 m) long, had a toothless beak and a crest on top of its light skull. With its hollow bones, long legs, and long, skinny feet, it was built for speed!

Gallimimus

Similar to an ostrich, *Gallimimus* had a slender neck and long legs that made it a fast runner. But unlike birds, which have a feathered tail and wings, it had a bony tail and arms tipped with clawed fingers.

Gallimimus had eyes on either side of its head, allowing it to spot danger from all sides. Paleontologists believe it was an herbivore, but its hooked claws would have allowed it to catch small animals.

Deinonychus

Known to be an aggressive, intelligent dinosaur, *Deinonychus* was a quick and voracious predator. It's believed that *Deinonychus* leaped on top of its prey, spreading its arms wide like a pair of wings. It probably used the long, terrifying claws on its feet to tear through flesh.

Troodon

This theropod had huge eyes, which suggests that it hunted at night. *Troodon*'s brain was proportionally bigger compared to its size, which is why paleontologists believe it was the most intelligent dinosaur of all.

Velociraptor

Velociraptor was a fast runner, but it had a big second claw on each foot that it had to keep raised when moving around. It used this claw to attack large prey. It had long fingers tipped with fearsome claws that it used to hold onto its food. It is thought to have been covered with down, or maybe even feathers.

BIG PREDATORS: THE POWERFUL THEROPODS

Tyrannosaurus rex

Tyrannosaurus rex has long been the biggest known carnivore. Its name means "king of the tyrant lizards." About 50 *Tyrannosaurus rex* skeletons have been found in North America, where it lived.

It had highly developed senses of smell, sight, and hearing. Unlike many other dinosaurs of its time, its eyes were located in the front of its head. This gave it excellent 3D vision, helping it to better spot its prey.

Tyrannosaurus rex was 38 feet (12 m) long and could weigh up to 5 tons.

Tyrannosaurus rex had powerful jaws. There were several holes in its skull, which scientists know were anchor points for the muscles that gave the dinosaur its colossal bite.

It had 60 sword-shaped teeth, 8 inches (20 cm) long and serrated like knife blades, that could easily cut through the hides of its prey.

Albertosaurus

This theropod is small compared to its cousin *Tyrannosaurus rex*—only 26 feet (8 m) long. Scientists believe that it could run up to 25 miles (40 km) per hour, which made it a fearsome hunter capable of chasing down its prey.

Its name comes from the province of Alberta, in Canada, where its fossilized remains were discovered!

Spinosaurus

Spinosaurus was bigger than *Tyrannosaurus rex*, but lighter. Its long, tapered jaw certainly made an impression, but it's best known for the huge spines on its back.

Giganotosaurus

Even bigger than the *Tyrannosaurus rex*, *Giganotosaurus* had a bony crest on its head and powerful arms. Its hands, tipped with serrated claws, were tailor-made for gripping onto its prey.

Carnotaurus

Head-on, *Carnotaurus* was a terrifying
sight to behold, with its massive jaw, sharp teeth,
and two horns above its eyes, which it used in combat.

Its arms were probably too small to hold onto its prey.

Therizinosaurus

This dinosaur had enormous claws: The claw on its first finger was longer
than an adult human's arm! It had a long neck and a small head
with a toothless beak. *Therizinosaurus* was bipedal, but slow and wobbly.

WEIRD HEADS: THE MARGINOCEPHALIANS

During the Cretaceous period, the skulls of some dinosaurs evolved to form bony growths. This explains all the weird-looking heads! These dinosaurs are known as the **marginocephalians**, a type of ornithischian dinosaur.

Triceratops

As its name implies, *Triceratops* had three horns: a smaller one on its nose and two others above its eyes. Even though it was an herbivore, its horns gave it an edge against predators.

Triceratops used its sharp, pointy beak to cut plants, which it then chewed with its sharp teeth.

Pentaceratops

Pentaceratops had five horns: one on its nose, two above its eyes, and two more on its cheeks. But that wasn't its most impressive feature: Its frill could grow up to 9 feet (2.7 m)—longer than a car!

Stygimoloch

This dinosaur had a domed head and bony horns that gave it a devilish look. Its name means "demon from the River Styx."

Styracosaurus

Styracosaurus had a massive nasal horn. The others, on the top of its head, pointed backward.

IN THE CRETACEOUS SKY

There were still many types of pterosaurs around during the Cretaceous period, although some of them evolved. They were still the masters of the sky, even though birds were increasing in number.

Pteranodon

A lot is known about this flying dinosaur because many fossils have been found. This pterosaur had a short tail and a long jaw, perfect for catching fish.

IN THE CRETACEOUS SEAS

Large predators were still swimming the seas during the Cretaceous period. Marine reptiles evolved but found themselves joined by other animals, including the earliest crocodiles and the ancestors of turtles.

Deinosuchus

Deinosuchus was not an ocean-dwelling species; it preferred to hunt down its prey in rivers. It was shaped like today's crocodiles and alligators, but was much bigger, growing up to 40 feet (12 m). In some places, it was definitely the biggest and most dangerous predator around.

Quetzalcoaltus

Quetzalcoaltus was the biggest flying animal that ever existed, and it lived during the Cretaceous period. This pterosaur was as tall as a giraffe and had the wingspan of a small airplane. Its prey quaked with fear at the sight of its deadly shadow! *Quetzalcoaltus* probably landed on all four legs when it swooped down to catch its food in its long toothless beak. Despite its immense size, it could move around quickly on the ground.

Pterodaustro

This pterosaur was known for its strange jaw and the long, thin teeth that lined its beak. Instead of chewing, it used its teeth to filter microscopic animals out of the water, a little like a baleen whale.

Mosasaurus

Mosasaurus was one of the last giant marine reptiles on record. With its pointed teeth and extremely powerful jaw, it was capable of biting through even the toughest of shells. Paleontologists believe that it may even be the ancestor of the Komodo dragon!

THE EXTINCTION OF THE DINOSAURS

The extinction of the dinosaurs is an event that is still shrouded in mystery. The most likely explanation is that a huge asteroid crashed into the Earth. A crater 125 miles (200 km) in diameter has even been found in Mexico to support this theory.

This would have happened about 65 million years ago. While it's not the biggest extinction event in Earth's history, it's certainly the most intriguing. After all, the huge dinosaurs of the Cretaceous period had nothing to fear. They were big, strong, powerful, and adapted to all kinds of environments. And yet, they disappeared.

After the asteroid hit, it's likely that the sun's light was blotted out and the water level in the oceans dropped significantly. A series of volcanic eruptions also probably happened. All these events, even if they took place over a long period of time, would have radically altered living conditions on Earth.

The smaller animals were better equipped to survive a disaster. They also needed less to survive. That's why insects, mammals, small reptiles, marine animals, and birds were able to survive the extinction event.

SUMMARY

In this book, you met...
Dinosaurs that lived on land:

Period	Dinosaur	Category	Type
TRIASSIC	*Coelophysis* (p. 18)	Saurischian	Ancestor of theropods
	Cynodontia (p. 21)	Saurischian	Ancestor of sauropodomorphs
	Eoraptor lunensis (p. 19)	Saurischian	Ancestor of theropods
	Plateosaurus (p. 20)	Saurischian	Ancestor of mammals
	Rhynchosaur (p. 21)	Saurischian	Ancestor of mammals
JURASSIC	*Albertosaurus* (p. 49)	Saurischian	Theropod
	Allosaurus (p. 31)	Saurischian	Theropod
	Apatosaurus (p. 29)	Saurischian	Sauropodomorph
	Brachiosaurus (p. 27)	Saurischian	Sauropodomorph
	Compsognathus (p. 32)	Saurischian	Theropod
	Cryolophosaurus (p. 33)	Saurischian	Theropod
	Diplodocus (p. 29)	Saurischian	Sauropodomorph
	Giraffatitan (p. 28)	Saurischian	Sauropodomorph
	Heterodontosaurus (p. 34)	Ornithischian	Ornithopod
	Kentrosaurus (p. 34)	Ornithischian	Thyreophoran
	Megalosaurus (p. 33)	Saurischian	Theropod
	Sauroposeidon (p. 28)	Saurischian	Sauropodomorph
	Scelidosaurus (p. 34)	Ornithischian	Thyreophoran
	Stegosaurus (p. 35)	Ornithischian	Thyreophoran
CRETACEOUS	*Carnotaurus* (p. 51)	Saurischian	Theropod
	Corythosaurus (p. 41)	Ornithischian	Ornithopod
	Deinonychus (p. 47)	Saurischian	Theropod
	Edmontosaurus (p. 42)	Ornithischian	Ornithopod
	Euoplocephalus (p. 44)	Ornithischian	Thyreophoran
	Gallimimus (p. 46)	Saurischian	Theropod
	Gastonia (p. 44)	Ornithischian	Thyreophoran
	Giganotosaurus (p. 50)	Saurischian	Theropod
	Iguanodon (p. 40)	Ornithischian	Ornithopod
	Maiasaura (p. 42)	Ornithischian	Ornithopod
	Oviraptor (p. 46)	Saurischian	Theropod

Period	Dinosaur	Category	Type
CRETACEOUS	*Parasaurolophus* (p. 43)	Ornithischian	Ornithopod
	Pentaceratops (p. 52)	Ornithischian	Marginocephalian
	Sauropelta (p. 45)	Ornithischian	Thyreophoran
	Spinosaurus (p. 50)	Saurischian	Theropod
	Stygimoloch (p. 53)	Ornithischian	Marginocephalian
	Styracosaurus (p. 53)	Ornithischian	Marginocephalian
	Therizinosaurus (p. 51)	Saurischian	Theropod
	Triceratops (p. 52)	Ornithischian	Marginocephalian
	Troodon (p. 47)	Saurischian	Theropod
	Tyrannosaurus rex (p. 48)	Saurischian	Theropod
	Velociraptor (p. 47)	Saurischian	Theropod

Dinosaurs that lived in the sky:

Period	Dinosaur	Category	Type
TRIASSIC	*Eudimorphodon* (p. 22)	Ornithischian	Prehistoric flying reptile
JURASSIC	*Archaeopteryx* (p. 36)	Ornithischian	Ancestor of birds
	Dimorphodon (p. 37)	Ornithischian	Prehistoric flying reptile
CRETACEOUS	*Quetzalcoaltus* (p. 55)	Ornithischian	Flying reptile
	Pteranodon (p. 54)	Ornithischian	Flying reptile
	Pterodaustro (p. 55)	Ornithischian	Flying reptile

Dinosaurs that lived in the seas:

Period	Dinosaur	Category	Type
TRIASSIC	*Ichthyosaur* (p. 23)	Saurischian	Prehistoric marine reptile
	Nothosaur (p. 22)	Saurischian	Prehistoric marine reptile
JURASSIC	*Ammonoids* (p. 36)	Saurischian	Cephalopod mollusk
	Plesiosaurus (p. 37)	Saurischian	Marine reptile
	Pliosaurus (p. 37)	Saurischian	Marine reptile
CRETACEOUS	*Deinosuchus* (p. 54)	Saurischian	Marine reptile
	Mosasaurus (p. 55)	Saurischian	Marine reptile

QUIZ

1. What was the name of the supercontinent that existed before the Triassic period?

a) Apogea   c) Pangaea

b) Plongea   d) Apartea

2. What does the name *Eoraptor lunensis* mean?

a) Egg thief   c) Amber thief

b) Spirit thief   d) Dawn thief

3. What did *Deinosuchus* look like?

a) A crocodile   c) A dolphin

b) A dog   d) A parrot

4. Which era of Earth's history is associated with the reign of the dinosaurs?

a) Precambrian era   c) Mesozoic era

b) Paleozoic era   d) Cenozoic era

5. What is the main characteristic of sauropodomorphs?

a) A long nose   c) Long claws

b) A long neck   d) Big ears

6. I was the smallest theropod of the Jurassic period. Who am I?

a) *Gallimimus*   c) *Compsognathus*

b) *Allosaurus*   d) *Cryolophosaurus*

7. What was the difference between brachiosaurs and diplodocids?

a) The shape of their tail   c) Their size

b) The length of their neck   d) The shape of their teeth

8. What type of dinosaur was *Tyrannosaurus rex*?

a) Ornithopod   c) Theropod

b) Thyreophoran   d) Sauropodomorph

9. I am a small herbivore with three types of teeth. Who am I?

a) *Heterodontosaurus*   c) *Allosaurus*

b) *Molarosaurus*   d) *Spinosaurus*

10. What was *Archaeopteryx* the first representative of?

a) Fish   c) Mammals

b) Marine reptiles   d) Birds

11. Approximately how many dinosaur species have been identified to date?

a) 90,000   c) 90

b) 9,000   d) 900

12. My nickname is the "cow of the Cretaceous period." Who am I?

c) *Stegosaurus*   c) *Parasaurolophus*

b) *Iguanodon*   d) *Styracosaurus*

QUIZ

13. What was the name of the dinosaur that took care of its young?

a) *Velociraptor*   c) *Mosasaurus*

b) *Pteranodon*   d) *Maiasaura*

14. Which of the following dinosaurs is not a saurischian?

a) *Sauroposeidon*   c) *Carnotaurus*

b) *Brachiosaurus*   d) *Triceratops*

15. Which defense mechanism was mainly used by ankylosaurids?

a) A club at the end   c) An unpleasant smell
of their tail

b) Venom   d) Poisonous claws

16. What odd characteristic did *Therizinosaurus* have?

a) A sail on its back   c) A claw longer
than a human arm

b) Eight toes on   d) Eyes bigger
each foot   than its hands

17. Finish this sentence: "*Troodon* was the _____ of all the dinosaurs."

a) Fastest   c) Most intelligent

b) Most agile   d) Most beautiful

18. Where does the name *Albertosaurus* come from?

a) The person who discovered   c) It was discovered
it was named Albert.   in Berto, Alabama.

b) It was discovered in Alberta.

19. Which of the following was not found in the Jurassic skies?

a) *Quetzalcoaltus*   c) *Pterodaustro*

b) *Pteranodon*   d) *Deinosuchus*

20. Which dinosaur was nicknamed the "demon from the River Styx?"

a) *Stygimoloch*   c) *Kentrosaurus*

b) *Oviraptor*   d) *Scelidosaurus*

21. What is thought to have caused the extinction of the dinosaurs?

a) The explosion of the Moon   c) The uprising
of the mammals

b) An asteroid that crashed
into Earth

22. Which of the following tools is not used by a paleontologist?

a) A hammer   c) A chainsaw

b) A needle   d) A scraper

23. What type of rock are most fossils found in?

a) Igneous   c) Metamorphic

b) Sedimentary

24. Where might *Coelophysis* have lived?

a) In the sea   c) In the desert plains

b) In the forest   d) In the marshes

1. c), 2. d), 3. a), 4. c), 5. b), 6. c), 7. d), 8. c), 9. a), 10. d), 11. d), 12. b), 13. d), 14. d), 15. a), 16. c), 17. c), 18. b), 19. d), 20. a), 21. b), 22. c), 23. b), 24. c)